Series: Simplified Engineering Approaches

Video Game Engine Development Guide

(Using Xilinx® SoC Board)

Volume 4
Edition 1

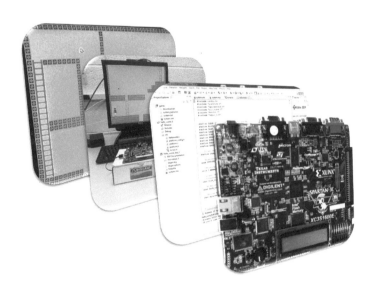

Ali Al-Bayaty

Video Game Engine Development Guide (Using Xilinx® SoC Board)

Available from Amazon.com, Amazon's European websites, CreateSpace.com, other book stores, other online stores, and other retail outlets.

Series: Simplified Engineering Approaches
Volume 4
Edition 1

First Published, 2017
Printed by CreateSpace, An Amazon.com Company
10 9 8 7 6 5 4 3 2 1

ISBN-13: 978-1976400940
ISBN-10: 1976400945

Dedication

To my *Soul* … my mother,
      For her prayers and patience.

To my *Mind* … my father,
      For his encouragement and advice.

To Prof. Christopher Martinez,
      For his academic supervision and guidance.

The number of transistors and resistors on a chip doubles every 18 months.

– Gordon Moore
Intel co-founder
(1965)

About the Author

Ali Al-Bayaty was born in Baghdad, Iraq, in 1981. He gained his B.Sc. in Computer Engineering and M.Sc. in Computer Engineering from Al-Nahrain University, in 2002 and 2005, respectively. He awarded the Fulbright Masters Scholarship to do his Graduate Certificate in Computer Programming and the M.S. in Electrical Engineering (MSEE) from the University of New Haven, Connecticut, USA in 2012 and 2014, respectively.

His research interests are focused on the computer vision techniques for biomedical engineering and robotic applications, and also on the Internet of Things (IoT) for robotics programming and localization through the SaaS approaches. He continued in the research field of computer engineering and focused on the mechatronics engineering and applications, computer vision and digital image processing, game engine, and visual programming language (VPL) for robotics.

He is currently working as an IT Coordinator at IRIS (Integrated Refugee & Immigrant Services), a federally recognized refugee resettlement agency in New Haven, Connecticut.

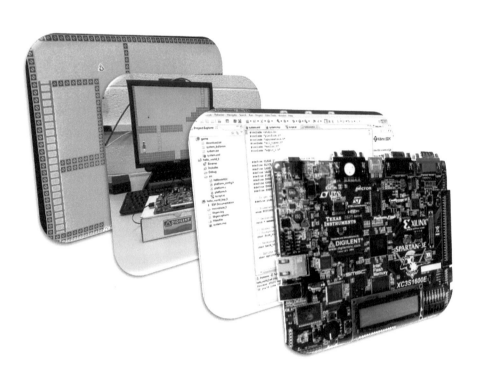

Table of Contents

List of Abbreviations

Abbreviation	Description
BRAM	Block RAM
CRT	Cathode Ray Tube
EDK	Embedded Development Kit
FBGA	Fine-Pitch Ball Grid Array
FPGA	Field Programmable Gate Array
FSM	Finite-State Machine
GPIO	General Purpose Input/Output
HSYNC	Horizontal Synchronization
IP	Intellectual Property
ISE	Integrated Synthesis Environment
LCD	Liquid Crystal Display
LED	Light-Emitting Diode
LUT	Look-Up Table
PLB	Processor Local Bus
VGA	Video Graphics Array
VGEP	Video Game Engine Project
VHDL	VHSIC Hardware Description Language
VHSIC	Very High Speed Integrated Circuit
VSYNC	Horizontal Synchronization
RGB	Red/Green/Blue Color Channels

SDK	Software Development Kit
SRAM	Static RAM
SoC	System-on-Chip
TBP	Timing Back Porch
TFP	Timing Front Porch
TPW	Timing Pulse Width
TTL	Transistor-Transistor Logic
UCF	User Constraints File
VESA	Video Electronics Standards Association

Preface

The increased numbers of self-developing 2D games, especially in the strategy, the platformer, and the role-playing games, by developers and engineers raises the needs to program and deploy these games into standalone and all-in-one devices, such as SoC (System-on-Chip) boards and smartphones, due to their powerful processing capabilities, compact sizes, and the availability of vast and different types of sensors as well.

This book is written and designed to spotlight and identify the basic concepts and the programming principles of developing a video game engine based on a SoC board, which is Spartan© 3E-1600 MicroBlaze® Development Board, using Nintendo® NES Gamepad (as a controller-action input device) and a standard VGA monitor (as a controller-response output device) as a completed and integrated project.

Finally, the completed work of this Video Game Engine Project (VGEP) in this book and its available online source-code can be used as a template project for developing different game engines that are based on the same characteristics of the game's characters (movements, actions, and weapons), the same monitor's coordinates, and the overall game logic by just re-filling specified graphical tile maps with the desirable drawing shapes and icons; as the fundamental approach that is currently used by many modern 2D games!

What This Book Covers

This book covers the development stages of VGEP as both hardware-based and software-based components using VHDL and C code, respectively, with the aid of Xilinx® programming environments and related platforms. It covers, also, the design and the implementation aspects of using Nintendo® NES Gamepad and a standard VGA monitor with their signaling and timing industrial-based specifications.

Moreover, the last two chapters of the book highlight the obtained results as FPGA (Field Programmable Gate Array) timing summaries and the future concluded notes of using such type of game engines development.

To Whom This Book Directed

Generally, the materials enclosed in this book will be a righteous guide to undergraduate students in Computer Science and Computer Engineering fields, and to the entry-level game engines developers using embedded systems deployment as well.

Source-Code Accessibility

The complete source-code of VGEP is freely available online and ready to be downloaded, used, and modified under the GNU GPL v3 License on the GitHub© Web page (https://github.com/albayaty/video-game-engine.git).

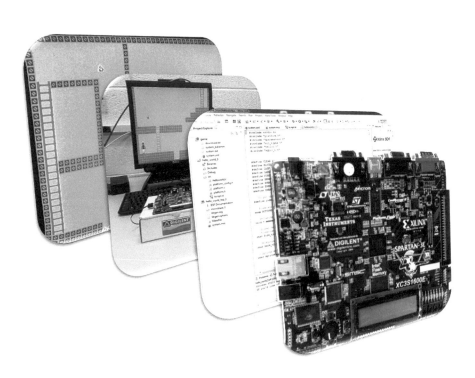

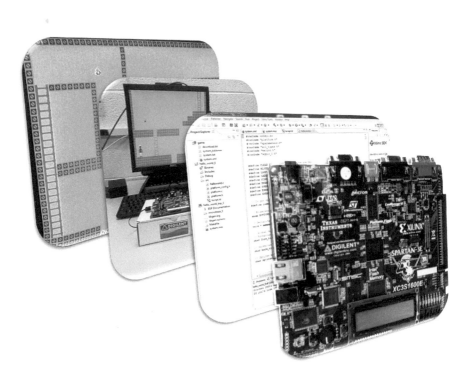

Chapter 1

Introduction

*) *) *)

Game Philosophy

The philosophy of developing VGEP (Video Game Engine Project) is based on creating a character, *Smurf*, that is able to move, jump, and throw *Strawberries*, as his weapon, in all of the directions in the game surrounding environment. There are two types of obstacles in the overall game surrounding environment, which are the *walls* and the *floors*. The walls prohibit Smurf from moving right or left when approaching them. Besides, the walls also prohibit Strawberries from passing-through them; and, they are smashed when touching the walls. While, the floors prevent Smurf from jumping upward and downward when there are no enough free spaces above or below, respectively. Moreover, the floors also prevent Smurf from the free-falling behavior, which is applied when Smurf steps over a hole in the floor. Thus, when there are clear spaces in the game surrounding environment, Smurf will be able to do all the types of the directional movements and jumps as well.

In the game surrounding environment, the *ladders* are special types of clear spaces that able Smurf to either climb up or climb down to different floors. And, these ladders are also considered as either an entrance to the next level (screen) or an exit to the previous level.

Totally, there are seven screens in the VGEP, six of them are considered as levels, while the screen number 7 is dedicated to displaying the *Winner* message after completing all the previous levels successfully!

In this VGEP, there are four types of enemies, which are *Ghosts*, *Bats*, *Bombs*, and *Fires*. These enemies are trying to hurt Smurf when there is a direct-touching behavior. And, Smurf is able to destroy them from a distance by throwing Strawberries on them, except Fires. The first three enemies are continuously moving in a horizontal, a vertical, or a diagonal direction in the game surrounding environment; and, the walls and the floors are considered as obstacles to them as well. Fires are considered as permanent enemies to Smurf since Strawberries are destroyed when direct-touching Fires. For that, Smurf can only jump over Fires, as an avoidance action. When anyone of the enemies is direct-touching Smurf, the game is over and Smurf's character transforms into an angelic character.

Development Scenario

The scenario of developing the VGEP is achieved with different approaches using the current state-of-the-art embedded technologies, such as SoC (System-on-Chip) development boards. This book has been prepared and designed to implement a stand-alone VGEP using Xilinx® FPGA (Field-Programmable Gate Array), as the control-action processing board, Nintendo® NES Gamepad, as the control-action input device as shown in Figure (1-1), and a VGA monitor, as the control-action output device.

The FPGA board, the NES Gamepad, and the VGA monitor are considered the hardware-based components of the VGEP.

Whereas, the software-based components can be divided into two modules, mainly: the first module is the game-controlling part that developed using C programming language, i.e. how Smurf, Strawberries, and the enemies are moving and acting in the game surrounding environment, while the second module is dedicated for controlling the hardware-based components using VHDL (VHSIC Hardware Description Language), i.e. how Smurf, Strawberries, and the enemies are being raster on the VGA monitor as well as handling the NES Gamepad's input signals. Each part of the hardware-based and the software-based components is divided into different modular sections, and then these modular sections are combined and connected together at the end to give the overall project meaning, which is the VGEP.

Figure (1-1) Nintendo® NES Gamepad.

The hardware-based components programming is implemented in Xilinx® ISE (Integrated Synthesis Environment) using VHDL, while the software-based components programming is implemented in Xilinx® SDK (Software Development Kit) with IP (Intellectual Property) cores using C code. Both the hardware-based and the software-based modular sections are implemented and tested using Spartan© 3E-1600 MicroBlaze® Development Board, as shown in Figure (1-2).

Figure (1-2) Spartan© 3E-1600 MicroBlaze® Dev. Board.

Design and Implementation Notes

Practically, the following VGEP's design and implementation notes are taken into account with careful considerations, which are:

- The interface between the FPGA board and the NES Gamepad is programmed via VHDL (hardware-based components), to read the status of the Gamepad's buttons and synchronize them to Xilinx® IP cores.

- The graphical components that are displayed on the VGA monitor are categorized into sprites (Smurf, Strawberries, and the enemies) and backgrounds (static objects, such as the walls, the floors, and the ladders), in the overall game surrounding environment.

- In order to get benefits of MicroBlaze® processing capability and get efficient memory space on Xilinx® FPGA board, the tile maps technique is used to reduce the overall board's memory size by differentiating and displaying the sprites and the backgrounds at the same time.

- The interfaces regarding the NES Gamepad and the displayed sprites/backgrounds within MicroBlaze® processor are connected together using the IP cores, which are generated using Xilinx® EDK (Embedded Development Kit) Platform Studio.

- The status of the NES Gamepad's pressed buttons is reflected to Spartan© 6-bit LEDs, as an indication of a successful input action.

- The BRAM (Block RAM) of the FPGA board is used instead of the LUT (Look-Up-Table) memory for storing the sprites and backgrounds, to increase the VGA monitor's resolution from (160×120) to (320×240) pixels.

- The levels of the overall game are called *screens* or *rotatable backgrounds* and they are loaded using the tile maps technique, which is invoked by using the NES Gamepad's buttons.

- In order to change the current screen to the next/previous one, there is a need for a large amount of memory to store the features of each screen; thus, the linked lists data structures for each graphical element in the designated screens are used to reduce the overall board's memory usage.

- Smurf (sprite) is moving in the game surrounding environment without affecting the static objects (backgrounds); since there are two tile maps: one for Background Map while the other is for Foreground Map, Smurf is drawn continuously on Foreground Map and keeping Background Map without any changes, especially after loading/rotating the screen(s).

- Smurf has the following movements: forward (moving to the right of the monitor), backward (moving to the left of the monitor), climbing ladders (moving upward and downward), and jumping (same location jump, left-jump, and right-jump).

- Customized timers are used in order to slow down the overall motions of sprites, as desired.

- The enemies (sprites) have the same characteristics as Smurf has, which are the data structures that build them, the linked lists that link them together with the other sprites, continuously drawn in Foreground Map, and their interactions with Smurf, Strawberries, and the overall game surrounding environment.

Figure (1-3) illustrates the used hardware-based components and the 'Level 1' screen of VGEP.

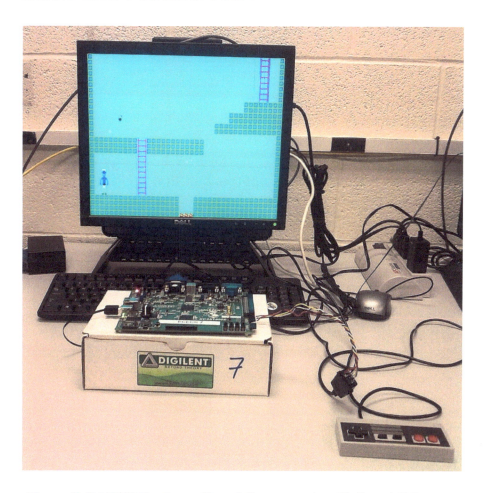

Figure (1-3) VGEP Hardware-Based Components with 'Level 1' Screen.

Aim of the Book

Basically, the main aim of this work is to design, develop, and implement a video game engine that is totally based on SoC using FPGA capabilities, Xilinx® programming platforms, Nintendo® NES Gamepad, VHDL, and C programming language for controlling the game project and interacting with it. The VGEP, also, gives the developers and the engineers to use this work as a template to build their own game engines to have the same characteristics, actions, and behaviors by only replacing the sprites and the backgrounds graphics, which is the fundamental used methodology in different strategy games.

Scope of the Book

The scope of the book is to cover the different technical methods and programming approaches that are used to build the completed and final VGEP version. Therefore, the general book structure will be categorized as follows:

- **Chapter 2** demonstrates the VGEP designing aspects for the used hardware-based and software-based components with their specifications.

- **Chapter 3** describes the VGEP implementation aspects using VHDL and C code within Xilinx® related products.

- **Chapter 4** illustrates the obtained results and different used methods with their timing summaries.

- **Chapter 5** states the achieved conclusions of VGEP as current notes and future development approaches.

Chapter 2

Design Aspects

Nintendo® NES Gamepad

The NES Gamepad has eight buttons, which are 'A', 'B', 'Select', 'Start', 'Up', 'Down', 'Left', and 'Right', that can be read using the signal termed 'nes_data', as an output data from the NES Gamepad to the FPGA board. When these eight buttons were pressed, the NES Gamepad generates a negative low output signal; thus, the FPGA board should invert these indications of the pressed buttons. The indicated pressed buttons are stored in a shift register inside the NES Gamepad before sending its signal to outside as the 'nes_data' signal. Besides, there are two input signals from the FPGA board to the NES Gamepad to control the synchronization of the pressed buttons and the output data as well, and these input signals termed as 'nes_latch' and 'nes_clk'. The 'nes_latch' signal is used first to fetch the button 'A' for 12 µs, and then the other seven buttons are fetched sequentially using the 'nes_clk' signal for 7 times on 12 µs period at 50% duty cycle.

Figure (2-1) illustrates the clock synchronization of the 'nes_latch' signal as the label 'Latch', the 'nes_clk' signal as the label 'Clock', and the labeled 'Data' is the fetched buttons' status from the NES Gamepad.

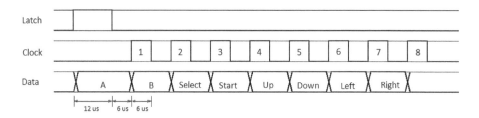

**Figure (2-1) Nintendo® NES Gamepad Clock Synchronization
(Source: spaces.usu.edu).**

The NES Gamepad is wired and directly connected to the FPGA board's 'J1' interface, as shown previously in Figure (1-1). And, the socket pinout of the NES Gamepad is illustrated as in Figure (2-2).

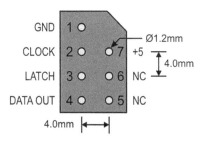

**Figure (2-2) Nintendo® NES Gamepad Socket Pinout
(Source: spaces.usu.edu).**

On the FPGA board side, the pins of the 'J1' interface are defined in the Xilinx® UCF (User Constraints File), as the following configuration:

```
NET "nes_latch" LOC = N15;        NET "led[0]"  LOC = D4;
NET "nes_clk"   LOC = N14;        NET "led[1]"  LOC = C3;
NET "nes_data"  LOC = E15;        NET "led[2]"  LOC = E6;
NET "reset"     LOC = N17;        NET "led[3]"  LOC = D6;
NET "clk_50"    LOC = C9;         NET "led[4]"  LOC = D13;
                                  NET "led[5]"  LOC = A7;
                                  NET "led[6]"  LOC = G9;
                                  NET "led[7]"  LOC = A8;
```

Technically, The FPGA board works at 50 MHz (20 ms), while the NES Gamepad deals with 12 µs period for the 'nes_latch' signal and 12 µsec period at 50% duty cycle for the 'nes_clk' signal.

The overall VGEP works using the FSM (Finite-State Machine) model; so, the program divided into two separated processes: the first process aims to calculate the frequency divider for both clocks of the 'nes_latch' and the 'nes_clk' signals, while the second process is dedicated to the state machines that check the NES Gamepad's eight buttons. And, Figure (2-3) illustrates the VGEP FSM model for both processes.

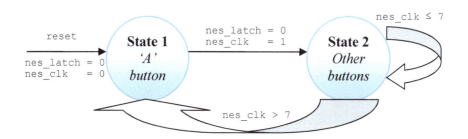

Figure (2-3) Nintendo® NES Gamepad FSM Model.

VGA Specifications

The Spartan© 3E FPGA board has a built-in VGA display port (DB15 connector) that gives the capability to connect most of the PC monitors and LCD displays using five VGA pins/signals, which are: R (Red), G (Green), B (Blue), HSYNC (Horizontal Sync), and VSYNC (Horizontal Sync). Each color line has a series resistor to provide a 3-bit color, with each 1-bit for 'R', 'G', and 'B' channels. The series resistor uses the 75Ω VGA cable termination to ensure that the color signals remain in the VGA-specified range (0.0 ~ 0.7 V). The 'HSYNC' and the 'VSYNC' signals are TTL levels. And, Spartan© 3E board's VGA specifications are illustrated as in Figure (2-4).

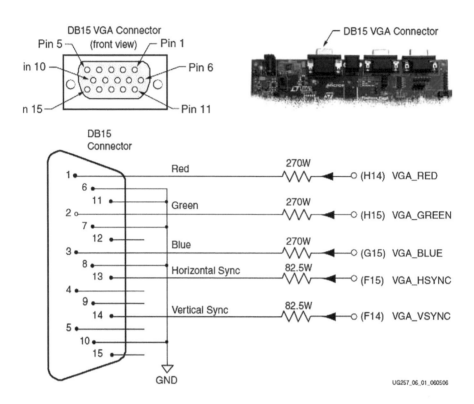

Figure (2-4) Spartan© 3E VGA Specifications
(Source: www.xilinx.com).

Driving 'R', 'G', and 'B' signals 'High' or 'Low' will generate eight possible colors combination, as stated in Table (2-1).

Table (2-1) The RGB Colors Combination.

Colors	R (Red)	G (Green)	B (Blue)
Black	0	0	0
Blue	0	0	1
Green	0	1	0
Cyan	0	1	1
Red	1	0	0
Magenta	1	0	1
Yellow	1	1	0
White	1	1	1

The VGA signaling and timing is specified, published, copyrighted, and sold by VESA (Video Electronics Standards Association). The following VGA system and timing information are provided as an example of how the FPGA board might drive VGA (CRT and LCD) monitors in (640×480) resolution. The CRT monitor uses an amplitude-modulated, moving electron beams (or cathode rays) to display information on a phosphor-coated screen. While, the LCD monitor uses an array of switches that can impose a voltage across a small amount of a liquid-crystal, thereby changing the light permittivity through the crystals is a pixel-by-pixel basis. Although the following description is limited to the CRT monitors, the LCD monitors have evolved to use the same signaling and timings as the CRT monitors do. Consequently, the following discussion pertains to both CRT and LCD monitors.

Within the CRT monitor, current-based waveforms pass through the coils to produce magnetic fields that deflect electron beams to transverse the monitor surface in a *raster* pattern, horizontally from left to right and vertically from top to bottom, as illustrated in Figure (2-5).

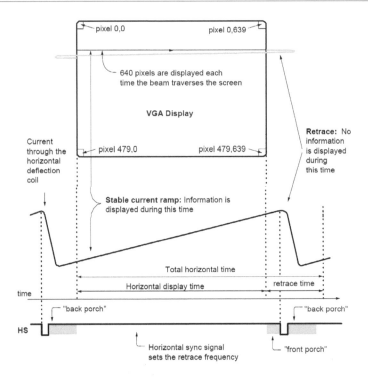

Figure (2-5) VGA Monitor Timing and Displaying Specifications (Source: www.xilinx.com).

Information is only displayed when the beam is moving in the *forward* direction (left to right and top to bottom) and not during the time the beam returns back to the left or the top edge of the monitor. Much of the potential display timing is, therefore, lost in the *blanking* periods, when the beam is reset and stabilized to begin a new horizontal or vertical display passing. The signal timings are derived for a 640-pixel by a 480-row display using a 25 MHz pixel clock at 60 Hz ±1 refresh rate. The timing for the sync pulse width (TPW) and front and back porch intervals (TFP and TBP) are based on observations from various VGA monitors. The front and back porch intervals are the pre-sync and the post-sync pulse times, and information cannot be displayed during these timings.

Regarding the VGEP, two VHDL files will be used: one for generating the required VGA signals, while the other for displaying the desirable data on the (640×480) monitor. The first file gives 'HSYNC' and 'VSYNC' signals to the monitor with the locations of the current pixel as '*pixel_x*' and '*pixel_y*' signals to the second file. Besides, the first file is responsible to generate the 25MHz clock from the FPGA board's clock; thus, there is no need for a frequency divider in the second file. And, the second file takes the current pixel locations and converts them to a 1D value, which will be used as an index to access the 2D tile map (20×15), as stated in (1).

$$index1 = (y \times Num\_Col) + x \tag{1}$$

Where,

index1   the index to access the 2D tile map,
Num_Col the number of columns of the 2D tile map,
x the mapping of the x-axis (as 640/*Num_Col*), and
y the mapping of the y-axis (as 480/*Num_Row*).

The used 2D tile map that forms the formal locations of the pixels on the monitor has 20 columns and 15 rows; thus, x and y can be formatted as in (2) and (3), respectively.

$$x = pixel\_x / 32 \tag{2}$$

$$y = pixel\_y / 32 \tag{3}$$

Therefore, the index can be rewritten as in (4).

$$index1 = (y \times 20) + x \tag{4}$$

And, this indexed 1D tile map is used to give the desired colors to the monitor through the RGB signal with the aid of the relationship between the two VHDL files, as illustrated in Figure (2-6).

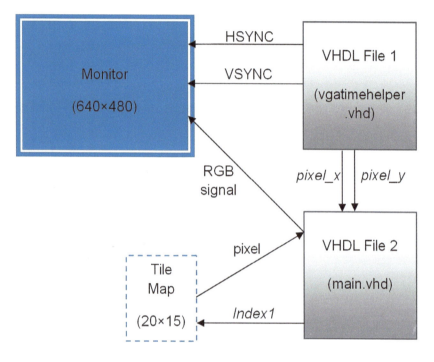

Figure (2-6) The VGA VHDL Files Relationship.

Tile Maps

In order to display the final pixels of objects (a collection of sprites and backgrounds) on the VGA monitor, there is a need for palettes to differentiate these objects, and so, they will not be interfered and over-written on each other. These palettes can be done using three different types of maps, and each map has the ability to draw its dedicated objects on the monitor. These three tile maps are *Foreground*, *Background*, and *Sprites*.

The Foreground Map consists of the objects that are represented as only as sprites above the backgrounds' objects; while the Background Map consists of different sets of static objects that are drawn behind the sprites. And, both Foreground and Background Maps are pointed to Sprites Map, which has the complete list of all sprites' and backgrounds' objects as sets of pixels. The Sprites Map consists of 32 rows and 64 columns, and each row represents an object as either a sprite or a background, while the columns represent the linear mapping of a 2D array of (8×8) pixels. Thus, the Sprites Map has 32 different VGEP's objects, and each object is represented by a linear 64 pixels (8×8).

In order to draw a pixel in a specific location on the VGA monitor with the provided information by either Foreground Map or Background Map, there is a need for an indexing approach that accesses each location separately and draws the accurate sets of pixels on the VGA monitor. The exact location and mapping from (640×480) monitor's resolution to (20×15) tile maps' resolution were given previously as in (4). For that, the locations of the sprites and the backgrounds in Sprites Map can be obtained by (5) and (6), respectively, based on the provided information of the given *index1*.

$$index2 = (pixel\_y \times 8) + pixel\_x + (Foreground[index1] \times 64) \quad (5)$$

$$index3 = (pixel\_y \times 8) + pixel\_x + (Background[index1] \times 64) \quad (6)$$

Now, after getting the indices of the objects (sprites and backgrounds) in Sprites Map, their contents of pixels are available and the decision of their drawing is based on the *transparency* bit (the 4th bit) in the object's pixel sets (the other three bits are the RGB channels). So, if the transparency bit is *clear* (0), means to draw the sprite's pixel regardless of the background's pixel, but if it's *set* (1), means to ignore the sprite's pixel and draw the background's pixel instead. And, the relationship of the two VGA VHDL files including the three tile maps are illustrated as in Figure (2-7).

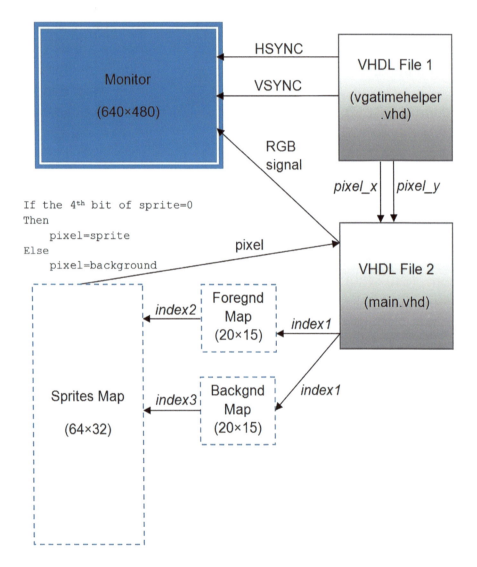

Figure (2-7) The VHDL Files and Tile Maps Relationship.

IP Cores

To control and manage the hardware-based components with C code, there is a need for the IP core that will be attached to the PLB (Processor Local Bus). This IP core is based on the VHDL files that control the overall system. And, these files have the appropriate hierarchical modules that operate in order, which are:

1. LAB.vhd: the essential file of the VGEP.

2. user_logic.vhd: creates and controls the signals and the registers from the 'LAB.vhd' file and passes them to the next file.

3. LAB_ip_core.vhd: creates the desirable IP core.

All the signals (ports) from the 'LAB.vhd' file are used as either registers, which are the communication channels between the hardware and C code through the PLB, or real hardware pins, which later be written in Xilinx® UCF that is generated and modified from the Xilinx® EDK Platform Studio. Then, two IP cores will be created, one for the VGA interface and the other for the NES Gamepad. The VGA part has some modifications in the original VHDL file, which are:

- Initially, the three tile maps are empty and will be filled with the required data using C code.

- Using the BRAM instead of the LUT memory by creating three separated processes without sensitivity lists.

21

- Changing the VGA monitor resolution from (160x120) (20×15 Foreground/Background Maps) to (320×240) (40×30 Foreground/Background Maps) by transforming from (4) to (7).

$$index1 = (y \times 40) + x \qquad (7)$$

Where,

$$x = pixel\_x / 16 \quad \text{(Mapping of x-axis, 640/40 = 16), and}$$
$$y = pixel\_y / 16 \quad \text{(Mapping of y-axis, 480/30 = 16).}$$

- Changing the indices of Sprites Map by transforming (5) to (8) and (6) to (9).

$$index2 = (pixel\_y \times 8) + pixel\_x + (foreground[index1] \times 64) \qquad (8)$$

$$index3 = (pixel\_y \times 8) + pixel\_x + (background[index1] \times 64) \qquad (9)$$

And the second IP core (NES Gamepad) does not have any changes in the original VHDL file, except that 8-bit LEDs will be 6-bit LED displays.

Table (2-2) shows the differences by using the signals (ports) in the original files and how to convert them in IP cores, either to registers or UCF; registers if there is a need for a storage space between VHDL and C code, and UCF for hardware-based pins.

Table (2-2) UCF and Registers in IP Cores.

IP Core	Port (VHDL)	Type	Register	UCF	Internal Signal
VGA Interface	clk	in: 1-bit			Bus2IP_Clk
	hsync	out: 1-bit		Yes	
	vsync	out: 1-bit		Yes	
	rgb	out: 3-bit		Yes	
	we	in: 1-bit	Yes		
	add_bus1	in: 11-bit	Yes		
	add_bus2	in: 11-bit	Yes		
	add_bus3	in: 11-bit	Yes		
	data_bus1	in: 5-bit	Yes		
	data_bus2	in: 5-bit	Yes		
	data_bus3	in: 4-bit	Yes		
	clk_50	in: 1-bit			Bus2IP_Clk
NES Gamepad	reset	in: 1-bit		Yes	
	led	out: 8-bit	Yes		
	nes_latch	out: 1-bit		Yes	
	nes_clk	out: 1-bit		Yes	
	nes_data	in: 1-bit		Yes	

Linked Lists Data Structure

In order to alternate between different screens, i.e. the levels of the VGEP, there is a need for different sets of Sprites Maps for each screen and different Background Maps as well. So, if such technique is used, then more memory is required for each screen that should have unique and separated Sprites and Background Maps. Contrary, the VGEP is implemented by rotating the screens with unified Sprites and Background Maps that are changed and reflected in each update of different screens; and, this can be done seamlessly by using the *linked lists* technique. Thus, each linked list can be represented by an individual *element* for a designated screen. So, if the first screen had three different drawing positions of the same sprite, then only one element is used for that repeated sprite.

The linked lists are programmed in the VGEP using C code in Xilinx® SDK with the following data structure:

```
struct element{
        char x, y;          // For x and y dimensions.
        char direction;     // Drawing Direction,
                            // 0:left-to-right, 1:up-to-down.
        char repeat;        // How many times to draw the
                            // same sprite.
        char sprite;        // The location of sprite in the
                            // Sprites Map.
        struct element* next;    // A pointer to the next
                                 // linked list's element.
};
```

Besides, there is another linked list for the consecutive screens, which is:

```
struct screen{
        struct element *head;   // Pointing to the first
                                // element in the same
                                // screen.
        struct screen *next;    // A pointer to next linked
                                // list's screen.
};
```

As a practice, to draw different six screens with different elements organization for each, the sequence of drawing these screens with their elements is implemented using the *counter* approach as the following steps:

1. Declaring and initializing the screens' counter to one.

2. Declaring Foreground Map and Background Map as (40×30) and without initialization.

3. Declaring and initializing Sprites Map of 32 objects.

4. Declaring and memory allocating the pointers of the structures (elements and screens).

5. Assigning the desirable data to the elements' structures to be displayed, and assigning these structures to the first screen's structure.

6. Loading the first screen.

7. Checking the pressed button(s) of the NES Gamepad. If it works, go to step (**7**) and increment the counter for the next screen; else keep checking.

8. Clearing the previous screen and its elements.

9. Go to step (**5**).

10. If the counter reaches the sixth screen and everything was well programmed, the practice is done!

To move the sprite (Smurf) in Foreground Map regardless of Background Map, there is a need for another drawing function to be used within Foreground Map only. This function works as the previous practice of drawing the screens from Background Map only, but this time, it will be used with Foreground Map. And, Smurf's structure is as the element's structure as mentioned previously. Because of Smurf consists of a number of sprites, which are ten sprites, the sequence of filling Smurf's structure is repeated for ten times. On the other hand, the function `constructor()` is implemented to achieve and simplify the operations of filling this structure with the required parameters and sprites (check **Chapter 3 'Implementation Aspects'** and the VGEP online source-code).

Since Smurf has customized movements and jumps in all directions of the game surrounding environment, the function `paintfgd()` plays double role of drawing and moving Smurf.

```
void paintfgd (struct element *units, int shiftx,
                            int shifty, int clear)
```

Where,

`units`   Smurf's linked list of the ten sprites.

`shiftx` 0 means there is no movement,
          (+ve) number means to move Smurf to the right, and
          (-ve) number means to move Smurf to the left.

`shifty` 0 means there is no movement,
          (+ve) number means to move Smurf downward, and
          (-ve) number means to move Smurf upward.

`clear`   1 means to clear Foreground Map to be used with the movements, while 0 means to append Smurf to Foreground Map without clearing Smurf and this is used when Smurf and the enemies are destroyed!

Movement Effects

In order to show the movement effects of Smurf, some sprites are continuously changed while Smurf is moving to the right and the left directions as well as the jumping. These effects are applied to Smurf's legs only, due to the limited memory resources of the FPGA board. Moreover, Smurf is always in the free-falling mode, and it stops when there is no clear sprite(s) below of Smurf in Background Map, i.e. there are floor's sprites.

In addition, Smurf has three different jumps, which are *jump-up*, *jump-right*, and *jump-left*. And, all of these different jumps are continuously testing three clear sprites around (above, right-side, and left-side) Smurf's sprites before performing any jumping type. For instance, if there were only two clear sprites above Smurf and after that there are floor's sprites, then Smurf's jump-up will be only two sprites upward instead of three.

Design Methodology

The VGEP's design methodology can be summarized and classified into two parts, which are:

I. Software Part

- Generating the 'nes_latch' signal of 12 µs period at 100% duty cycle.

- Generating the 'nes_clk' clock of 12 µs period at 50% duty cycle.

- The VHDL files are based on the FSM model in order to detect the NES Gamepad's buttons.

- The 25 MHz VGA clock is generated from VGA VHDL File 1; so, the main VHDL file is only dealing with the three tile maps (faster processing and handling).

- Converting the indices of 2D arrays into 1D vectors to access the three tile maps (faster access with fewer variables).

- Minimizing the number of lines in the main VHDL file, due to the simplified formulae (7), (8), and (9).

- Filling the three tile maps and memory spaces at the beginning of the software.

- Using the IP core's registers to communicate with the hardware, instead of C code variables.

- Declaring Foreground and Background Maps only, without initialization.

- Declaring and initializing Sprites Map only.

- Using the same linked lists structure for the screen, Smurf, Strawberries, and the enemies yields to less memory usage.

II. Hardware Part

- Both the 'nes_latch' and the 'nes_clk' signals are generated from the system clock of 50MHz.

- Interfacing the NES Gamepad with the FPGA board using the board's 'J1' pins.

- The FPGA board's 6 LEDs work as indications to the pressed buttons of the NES Gamepad.

- Accessing the three tile maps with mathematical formulae yields to an ease of manipulations, but with a complex FPGA generated hardware.

- Using small tile maps in order to reduce the overall amount of Xilinx® memory space.

- Interfacing the VGA monitor directly to Xilinx® VGA port using the board's built-in VGA pins.

- Using BRAMs to store the three tile maps, and reducing the size of the LUT memory as well.

- Changing the VGA monitor resolution from (160×120) to (320×240).

- Using the NES Gamepad's arrows to change Smurf's movement directions, 'A' button to throw Strawberries, 'B' button to jump, 'SELECT' button to reload the same screen (level), and 'START' button to reload the first screen.

- Using the NES Gamepad's 'Right' and 'Left' arrows to move Smurf to the right and the left directions, respectively; the 'Up' and the 'Down' arrows are used to climb the ladders upward or downward, respectively.

Chapter 3

Implementation Aspects

〈〉 〈〉 〈〉

Introduction

The VGEP is programmed and implemented, in total, using Xilinx® development kits. Two specific languages are used to differentiate the programming purposes based on their powerful and supported libraries regarding the project's demands and requirements, which are:

- VHDL (*VHDL 2000*) using Xilinx® ISE, and

- C (*C99*) using Xilinx® SDK.

The NES Gamepad is connected to the FPGA board using the IP cores that are generated from Xilinx® EDK Platform Studio.

Together, Xilinx® ISE, SDK, and EDK generated source-codes are implemented and tested using Spartan© 3E-1600 MicroBlaze® Development Board.

The complete source-code of the VGEP is freely available online and ready to be downloaded, used, and modified under the GNU GPL v3 License on the GitHub© Web page (https://github.com/albayaty/video-game-engine.git).

The online source-code files are categorized and grouped under different folders, which are representing their Xilinx® related products, as shown in Figure (3-1). And, these Xilinx® products can be downloaded and/or purchased using either Student or Commercial License(s) from Xilinx® Web site (http://www.xilinx.com/).

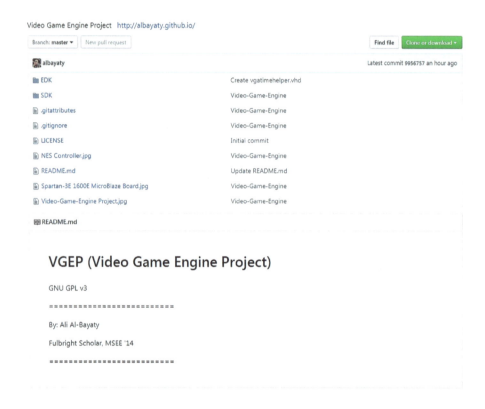

Figure (3-1) The VGEP Online Source-Code
(Source: github.com/albayaty/video-game-engine).

Source-Code Classifications

The VGEP source-code files are classified as two parts as the following:

- **Hardware Part (VHDL):**
  NES Gamepad implementation
  Interfacing GPIO (General Purpose Input/Output):
  - **A.** No-device driver
  - **B.** Low-level Driver
  - **C.** High-level driver

  Interfacing with Timer IP core
  Interfacing with Timer IP core using Interrupts
  VGATimeHelper.vhd (screen(s) coordination and
  clock generation)
  VGAMain.vhd (locations of sprites and backgrounds
  in Sprites Map)

  VGA IP core
  NES Gamepad IP core
  Xilinx® UCF

- **Software Part (C code):**

```
Global variables
MACROs
Foreground Map (40×30): characters
Background Map (40×30): screens (levels)
Sprites map (64×32): sprites and backgrounds
Structure of elements
Structure of screens
Filling up the BRAMs
Functions: initializations, clearing, and
          filling the elements and structures
Functions: sprites' different movements
main() { … }
```

33

Implementation Methodology

The VGEP's implementation methodology can be summarized as follows:

- Taking the advantage of the frequency divider technique to generate the desirable clocks.

- To make the VGEP simpler and without extra signals (less hardware), the 'nes_latch' and the 'nes_clk' signals are changed to IN and OUT mode.

- To make the VGEP simpler and without extra signals (less hardware), only the equations and output signals are used in VHDL main file (without PROCESS).

- There is no need for PROCESS statements in VHDL main file since everything works in combinational logic and not sequential logic.

- Using CASE statements instead of IF statements to decrease the complexity of the FPGA generated hardware.

- Because of the bitwise shifting is considered as an operation and required more hardware to be achieved, direct selections of bits are designed for the 'pixel_x' and the 'pixel_y' signals.

- Optimizing the overall program by using one FOR loop to fill the three tile maps.

- Instead of using the mathematical divisions in (8) and (9) as in Chapter 2, direct bits mapping is used to reduce the FPGA generated hardware.

- Most of the variables in C code are global, in order to manage the memory size of the SRAM (Static RAM).

- Separating the drawing and the clearing operations regarding the screens and the sprites as two functions, one for Foreground Map while the other for Background Map.

- Using a desirable FOR loop as a global timer for the overall game yields to less FPGA hardware usage.

- Using a desirable FOR loop as a delay for Strawberries smashing when touching the walls and the enemies.

Chapter 4

Results and Summaries

(5 (5 (5

Connecting Components

After configuring and connecting all of the hardware-based and the software-based components together to get the final implemented version of the VGEP, their results and summaries are as the following:

- Initiating the FPGA board's 'Reset' button to reset the two VHDL-related processes: the frequency divider and the FSM.

- All of the FPGA board's LEDs are 'ON' when the NES Gamepad is not connected to it, i.e. all of the FSM's states are working properly after inverting the zero level inputs (open) to 'ON'.

- When the NES Gamepad is connected to the FPGA board, the board's LEDs are working properly according to the 'nes_latch' signal, the 'nes_clk' signal, and the NES Gamepad fetched buttons. And, these buttons are fetched in a repeated sequence as follows.

  (A➜B➜Select➜Start➜Up➜Down➜Left➜Right).

- **VGEP Timing Summary:**
  Speed Grade: -4,
  Min. period: 8.270 ns (max. freq.: 120.917 MHz),
  Min. input arrival time before clock: 3.385 ns,
  Max. output required time after clock: 4.368 ns, and
  Max. combinational path delay: No path found.

- The overall project works properly for the three different equivalent methods, as they are stated in Table (4-1).

Table (4-1) The Results of Equivalent Methods.

Method	No. of 4-Input LUT	No. of Occupied Slices
1. Using Formula (7)	117	73
2. Replacing Division by Shifting	117	73
3. Replacing Shifting by Direct-Bit Wiring	113	71

Methods Timing Summary:
  Speed Grade: -4,
  (*Methods 1 and 2*):
    Min. period: 5.449 ns (max. freq.: 183.520 MHz),
    Max. output required time after clock: 18.420 ns,
  (*Method 3*):
    Min. period: 5.689 ns (max. freq.: 175.783 MHz), and
    Max. output required time after clock: 13.837 ns.

- The project works properly by drawing the sprites without overlapping within the backgrounds. And, the results are the same for both methods, as stated in Table (4-2).

Table (4-2) The Results of Sprites Methods.

Method	No. of 4-Input LUT	No. of Occupied Slices
1. Normal Division	511	323
2. Replacing Division by Direct-Bit Wiring	511	323

Methods Timing Summary:

Speed Grade: -4,

Min. period: 5.897 ns (max. freq.: 169.584 MHz),

Min. input arrival time before clock: No path found,

Max. output required time after clock: 20.755 ns, and

Max. combinational path delay: No path found.

- The project works properly with the desirable results for the VGA and the NES Gamepad IP cores. The results can be demonstrated as in Figure (4-1), Figure (4-2), Figure (4-3), Figure (4-4), Figure (4-5), and Figure (4-6) with their timing summaries.

Device Utilization Summary					[-]
Logic Utilization	Used	Available	Utilization	Note(s)	
Number of Slice Flip Flops	33	29,504	1%		
Number of 4 input LUTs	2,388	29,504	8%		
Number of occupied Slices	1,218	14,752	8%		
Number of Slices containing only related logic	1,218	1,218	100%		
Number of Slices containing unrelated logic	0	1,218	0%		
Total Number of 4 input LUTs	2,406	29,504	8%		
Number used as logic	984				
Number used as a route-thru	18				
Number used for Dual Port RAMs	1,404				
Number of bonded IOBs	50	250	20%		
Number of BUFGMUXs	1	24	4%		
Average Fanout of Non-Clock Nets	6.46				

Figure (4-1) VGA (160×120) Device Utilization Summary.

```
    Synthesizing Unit <vga>.
        Related source file is "C:/proj5/vga/main.vhd".
⚠WARNING:Xst:653 - Signal <reset> is used but never assigned. This sourceless signal '
⚠WARNING:Xst:646 - Signal <pixel_y<1:0>> is assigned but never used. This unconnected
⚠WARNING:Xst:646 - Signal <pixel_x<1:0>> is assigned but never used. This unconnected
⚠WARNING:Xst:646 - Signal <index2<31:11>> is assigned but never used. This unconnecte
⚠WARNING:Xst:646 - Signal <index1<31:11>> is assigned but never used. This unconnecte
⚠WARNING:Xst:646 - Signal <index<31:9>> is assigned but never used. This unconnected
        Found 300x5-bit dual-port RAM <Mram_back_map> for signal <back_map>.
        Found 2048x4-bit dual-port RAM <Mram_sprites> for signal <sprites>.
        Found 2048x4-bit dual-port RAM <Mram_sprites_ren> for signal <sprites>.
        Found 300x5-bit dual-port RAM <Mram_fore_map> for signal <fore_map>.
        Found 10-bit adder for signal <index$add0000> created at line 112.
        Found 5x5-bit multiplier for signal <index$mult0000> created at line 112.
        Found 11-bit adder for signal <index1$add0000> created at line 114.
        Found 11-bit adder for signal <index2$add0000> created at line 117.
        Found 6-bit adder for signal <index2$add0001> created at line 117.
        Summary:
            inferred   4 RAM(s).
            inferred   4 Adder/Subtractor(s).
            inferred   1 Multiplier(s).
    Unit <vga> synthesized.


    ============================================================================
    ┌──────┐
  ◄ │ III  │                                                                 ►
    └──────┘
    ┌─────────────────┐
    │        ☒        │
    └─────────────────┘
```

Figure (4-2) VGA (160×120) BRAM Components.

Timing Summary:

Speed Grade: -4,

Min. period: 5.939 ns (max. freq.: 168.392 MHz),

Min. input arrival time before clock: 5.971 ns,

Max. output required time after clock: 18.930 ns, and

Max. combinational path delay: No path found.

Device Utilization Summary				[-]
Logic Utilization	Used	Available	Utilization	Note(s)
Number of Slice Flip Flops	27	29,504	1%	
Number of 4 input LUTs	4,019	29,504	13%	
Number of occupied Slices	2,046	14,752	13%	
Number of Slices containing only related logic	2,046	2,046	100%	
Number of Slices containing unrelated logic	0	2,046	0%	
Total Number of 4 input LUTs	4,042	29,504	13%	
Number used as logic	1,495			
Number used as a route-thru	23			
Number used for Dual Port RAMs	2,524			
Number of bonded IOBs	54	250	21%	
Number of BUFGMUXs	1	24	4%	
Number of MULT18X18SIOs	1	36	2%	
Average Fanout of Non-Clock Nets	6.76			

Figure (4-3) VGA (320×240) Device Utilization Summary.

```
Synthesizing Unit <vga>.
    Related source file is "C:/proj5/vga/main.vhd".
⚠WARNING:Xst:653 - Signal <reset> is used but never assigned. This sourceless signal
⚠WARNING:Xst:646 - Signal <pixel_y<0>> is assigned but never used. This unconnected s
⚠WARNING:Xst:646 - Signal <pixel_x<0>> is assigned but never used. This unconnected s
⚠WARNING:Xst:646 - Signal <index2<31:11>> is assigned but never used. This unconnecte
⚠WARNING:Xst:646 - Signal <index1<31:11>> is assigned but never used. This unconnecte
⚠WARNING:Xst:646 - Signal <index<31:11>> is assigned but never used. This unconnected
    Found 1200x5-bit dual-port RAM <Mram_back_map> for signal <back_map>.
    Found 2048x4-bit dual-port RAM <Mram_sprites> for signal <sprites>.
    Found 2048x4-bit dual-port RAM <Mram_sprites_ren> for signal <sprites>.
    Found 1200x5-bit dual-port RAM <Mram_fore_map> for signal <fore_map>.
    Found 12-bit adder for signal <index$add0000> created at line 109.
    Found 6x6-bit multiplier for signal <index$mult0000> created at line 109.
    Found 11-bit adder for signal <index1$add0000> created at line 111.
    Found 11-bit adder for signal <index2$add0000> created at line 114.
    Found 6-bit adder for signal <index2$add0001> created at line 114.
    Summary:
        inferred    4 RAM(s).
        inferred    4 Adder/Subtractor(s).
        inferred    1 Multiplier(s).
Unit <vga> synthesized.
```

```
◄   III                                                                  ►
   [ ] Σ              Design Summary                    [X]
```

Figure (4-4) VGA (320×240) BRAM Components.

Timing Summary:

Speed Grade: -4,

Min. period: 10.869 ns (max. freq.: 92.002 MHz),

Min. input arrival time before clock: 6.356 ns,

Max. output required time after clock: 25.879 ns, and

Max. combinational path delay: No path found.

Device Utilization Summary					[-]
Logic Utilization	Used	Available	Utilization	Note(s)	
Total Number Slice Registers	70	29,504	1%		
Number used as Flip Flops	69				
Number used as Latches	1				
Number of 4 input LUTs	131	29,504	1%		
Number of occupied Slices	91	14,752	1%		
Number of Slices containing only related logic	91	91	100%		
Number of Slices containing unrelated logic	0	91	0%		
Total Number of 4 input LUTs	167	29,504	1%		
Number used as logic	131				
Number used as a route-thru	36				
Number of bonded IOBs	13	250	5%		
IOB Latches	8				
Number of BUFGMUXs	1	24	4%		
Average Fanout of Non-Clock Nets	3.48				

Figure (4-5) NES Gamepad Device Utilization Summary.

Timing Summary:

Speed Grade: -4,

Min. period: 8.270 ns (max. freq.: 120.917 MHz),

Min. input arrival time before clock: 3.385 ns,

Max. output required time after clock: 4.368 ns, and

Max. combinational path delay: No path found

Device Utilization Summary (actual values)				[-]
Logic Utilization	Used	Available	Utilization	Note(s)
Total Number Slice Registers	3,044	29,504	10%	
Number used as Flip Flops	3,035			
Number used as Latches	9			
Number of 4 input LUTs	5,729	29,504	19%	
Number of occupied Slices	4,667	14,752	31%	
Number of Slices containing only related logic	4,667	4,667	100%	
Number of Slices containing unrelated logic	0	4,667	0%	
Total Number of 4 input LUTs	5,908	29,504	20%	
Number used as logic	3,859			
Number used as a route-thru	179			
Number used for Dual Port RAMs	1,724			
Number used as Shift registers	146			
Number of bonded IOBs	66	250	26%	
IOB Flip Flops	31			
IOB Master Pads	1			
IOB Slave Pads	1			
Number of ODDR2s used	22			
Number of RAMB16s	21	36	58%	
Number of BUFGMUXs	5	24	20%	
Number of DCMs	2	8	25%	
Number of BSCANs	1	1	100%	
Number of MULT18X18SIOs	3	36	8%	
Average Fanout of Non-Clock Nets	4.02			

Figure (4-6) EDK Platform Studio (IP Cores) Device Utilization Summary.

- The project works properly as planned for Smurf's movements and its action, e.g. throwing Strawberries. Different movements are tested with different combinations by pressing the designated buttons of the NES Gamepad. Besides, different sprites of Smurf's legs are associated with the specified movements.

- The four types of enemies are displayed and tested for each screen, and each type of these enemies has its own sprites and defined directional (horizontal, vertical, or diagonal) movement.

- Six screens (levels) are tested and worked in perfect as desired, plus the seventh screen is an indication of completing and winning the game.

Finally, Figure (4-7), Figure (4-8), Figure (4-9), Figure (4-10), and Figure (4-11) illustrate the different screens of the VGEP.

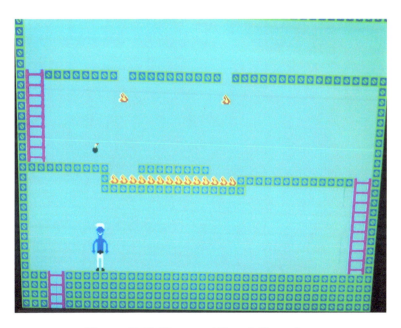

Figure (4-7) Fires and Bomb Enemies.

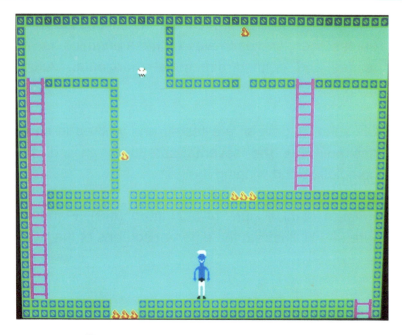

Figure (4-8) Fires and Ghost Enemies.

**Figure (4-9) Indication of Losing the Game
(When Touching Enemies, i.e. Fires).**

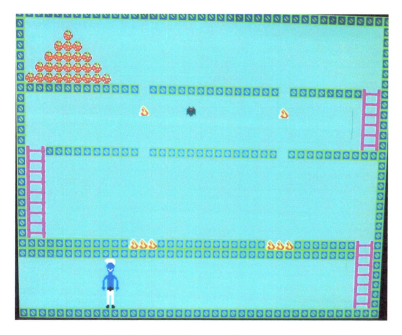

Figure (4-10) The Final Level with Prize (Screen #6).

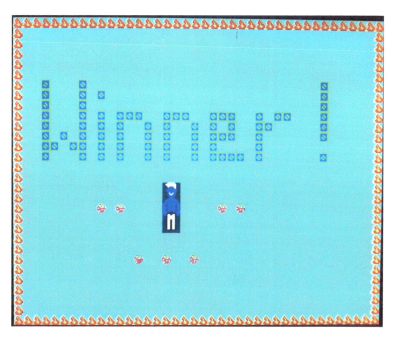

Figure (4-11) Indication of Winning the Game (Screen #7).

45

Chapter 5

Conclusions

*) *) *)

Notes

The following notes are obtained as conclusions for the completed VGEP work, and they can be used as instructions for further game engines development using Xilinx® related products, VHDL, and C code, which are:

- Getting the knowledge and how-to-use the SoC and other embedded systems using Xilinx® programming environments and platforms.

- Getting the knowledge about Nintendo® NES Gamepad and how to connect it to the FPGA board (Spartan© 3E-1600 MicroBlaze® Development Board).

- Manipulate the FPGA board's LEDs using VHDL and Xilinx® UCF.

- Generate two output clocks from the FPGA board to the NES Gamepad using the frequency divider of 25 MHz.

- Manipulate Xilinx® GPIO using three levels of interfacing: No-Device Driver, Low-Level Driver, and High-Level Driver.

- Associating the FSM model with the FPGA board's generated clocks in the real-time to synchronize the incoming data from the NES Gamepad and converting them as outputs using the board's LEDs.

- Using FOR loops as timing delay counters.

- Using the Timer IP core as a timing delay counter in the overall program with any of the three levels of Xilinx® GPIO interfacing.

- Interfacing the Timer IP core with Interrupts and re-initiate all the required procedures inside the ISRs (Interrupt Service Routines).

- Mapping from the three tile maps' coordinates to the VGA monitor's real coordinates.

- Getting the knowledge about how to apply mathematical formulae and their effects on Xilinx® hardware using normal divisions, bitwise shifting, and direct-bit mapping techniques.

- Developing three derived methods from the same mathematical formula in order to reduce the generated hardware, the LUT, and the slices in the FPGA board.

- The overall design is based on the combinational logic.

- Mapping from the three tile maps' indices to the desirable contents of Sprites Map (sprites and backgrounds).

- All of the three tile maps are becoming LUTs and not memory spaces (RAM).

- Increasing the VGA monitor resolutions from (160×120) to (320×240).

- Being able to choose sufficient memory sizes of SRAM by using the global variables in C code.

- The hardware-based of the VGA output is based on the combinational logic and not on the processes.

- Using the linked lists data structure of the elements for one screen and differentiating them from other screens.

- Using a unified linked list data structure regarding the screen's elements, Smurf, Strawberries, and the enemies.

- Initializing Foreground Map and Background Map on demand.

- Using a defined FOR loop as a timer.

- Separating the drawing and clearing of the screens and the sprites as two functions, one is for Foreground Map, while the other one is for Background Map.

- Implementing the hardware-based part of the project using VHDL and the software-based part using C code.

- Using the NES Gamepad's arrows to change the moving directions of Smurf, 'A' button to throw Strawberries, 'B' button to jump, 'SELECT' button to reload the same screen (level), and 'START' button to reload the first screen.

- Using MACROs as variables replacement and names representation regarding the colors, Smurf, Strawberries, and the three types of enemies using C code.

- Using the inline MACRO as a function replacement for the repeated expressions and actions along the C code.

- Terminating the destroyed Strawberries and the enemies from their linked lists data structure, in order to decrease the overall delay timing Foreground Map.

Finally, this VGEP can be used as a template project for developing different game engines that are based on the same characteristics of the sprites' movements/actions/weapons, the same monitor's coordinates, and the overall game logic by just re-filling Foreground, Background, and Sprites Maps with the desirable drawing shapes and icons; as the fundamental approach that is currently used by many modern 2D games!

Spartan© 3E-1600 MicroBlaze® Development Board Specifications

*) *) *)

Key Features and Components

- Xilinx® XC3S1600E Spartan© 3E FPGA:
  - Up to 250.
  - User-I/O pins.
  - 320-pin FBGA package.
  - Over 33,000 logic cells.
- Two Xilinx® 4 Mbit Platform Flash configuration PROM.
- Xilinx® 64-macrocell XC2C64A CoolRunner CPLD.
- 64 MByte (512 Mbit) of DDR SDRAM, x16 data interface, 100+ MHz.
- 16 MByte (128 Mbit) of parallel NOR Flash (Intel® StrataFlash):
  - FPGA configuration storage.
  - MicroBlaze® code storage/shadowing.
- 16 Mbits of SPI serial Flash (STMicro).
- FPGA configuration storage.
- MicroBlaze® 32-bit embedded RISC processor.
- MicroBlaze® code shadowing.
- 2×16 LCD display screen.
- PS/2 mouse or keyboard port.
- VGA display port.

- 10/100 Ethernet PHY (requires Ethernet MAC in FPGA).
- Two 9-pin RS-232 ports (DTE- and DCE-style).
- On-board USB FPGA/CPLD download/debug interface.
- 50 MHz and 66 MHz clock oscillators.
- SHA-1 1-wire serial EEPROM for bitstream protection.
- Hirose FX2 expansion connector with 40-user I/O.
- Three Digilent® 6-pin expansion connectors.
- Four-output, SPI-based DAC.
- Two-input, SPI-based ADC with programmable-gain.
- ChipScope™ SoftTouch debugging port.
- Rotary-encoder with push-button shaft.
- Eight discrete LEDs.
- Four slide switches.
- Four push-button switches.
- SMA clock input.
- 8-pin DIP socket for auxiliary clock oscillator.

**Figure (A-1) Xilinx® XC3S1600E Spartan© 3E MicroBlaze® Dev. Board
(Source: www.xilinx.com).**

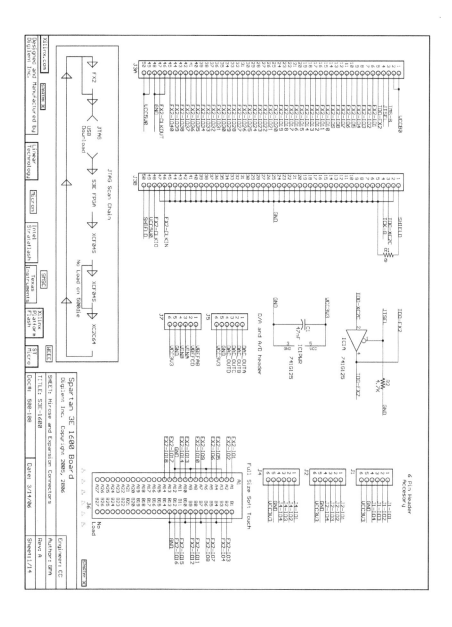

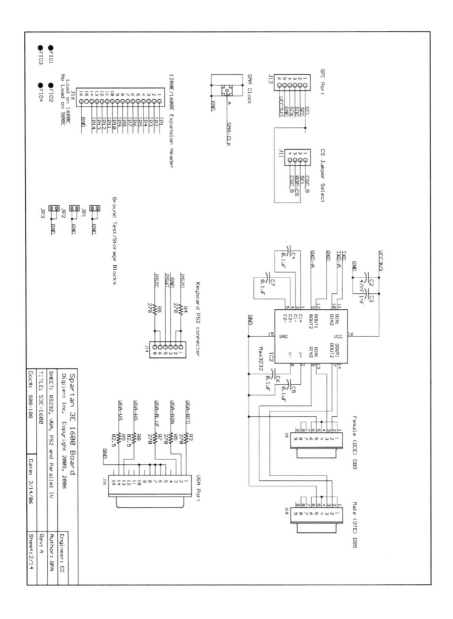

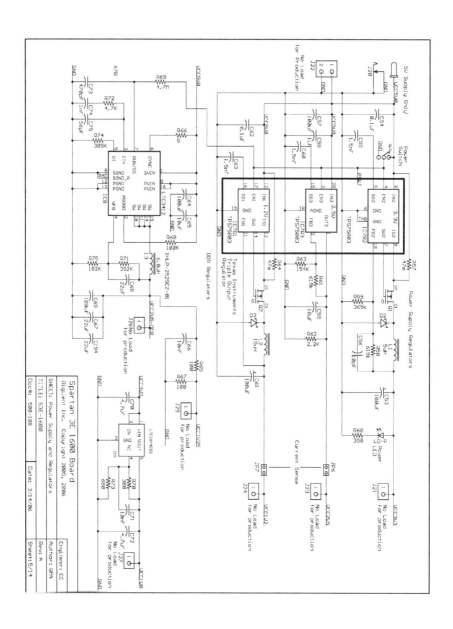

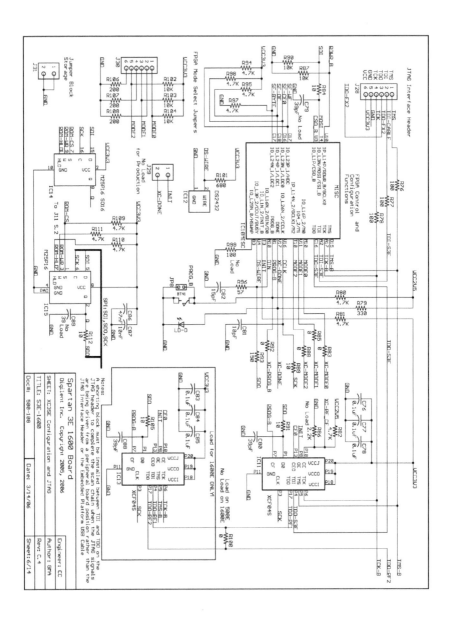

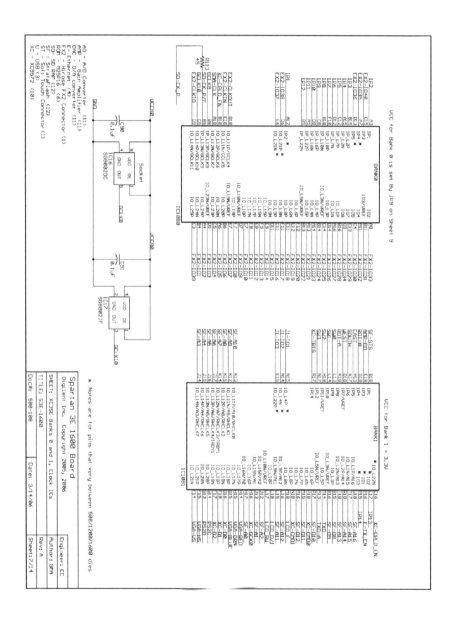

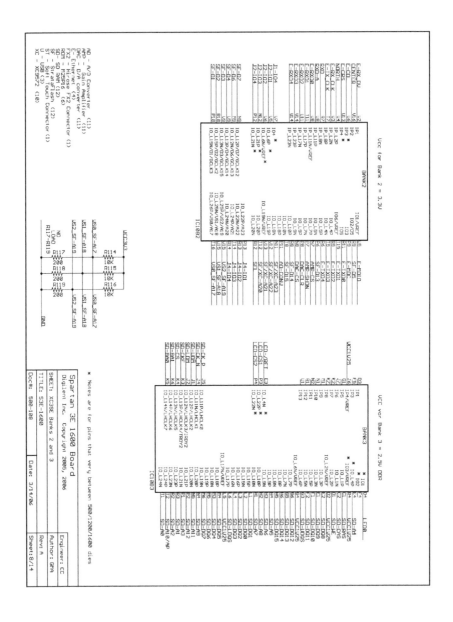

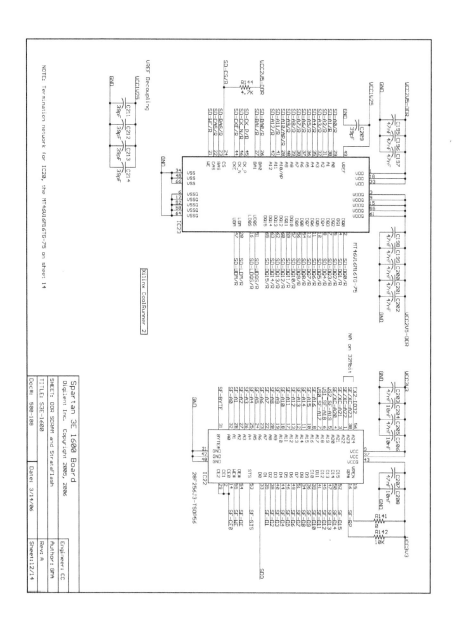

DDR Series Termination

Signal	Resistor	Value	Signal
SD-DQ0	R159	75	SD-A1 / SD-A1/R
SD-DQ1	R160	75	SD-A1/R
SD-DQ1	R161	75	SD-A2/R
SD-DQ2	R162	75	SD-A3/R
SD-DQ3	R163	75	SD-A4/R
SD-DQ4	R164	75	SD-A5/R
SD-DQ5	R165	75	SD-A6/R
SD-DQ6	R166	75	SD-A7/R
SD-DQ7	R167	75	SD-A8/R
SD-DQ8	R168	75	SD-A9/R
SD-DQ9	R169	75	SD-A10/NP/R
SD-DQ10	R170	75	SD-A11/R
SD-DQ11	R171	75	SD-A12/R
SD-DQ12	R172	75	SD-BA0/R
SD-DQ13	R173	75	SD-BA1/R
SD-DQ14	R174	75	SD-CKE/R
SD-DQ15	R175	75	SD-CS/R
SD-LDQS	R176	45	SD-RAS/R
SD-UDQS	R177	45	SD-CAS/R
SD-LDM	R178	45	SD-WE/R
SD-UDM	R179	45	
SD-WE	R180	45	SD-CK_P/R
	R181 150 No Load		SD-CK_N/R
SD-CK_P	R192 45		
SD-CK_N			

FX2 Differential Termination
Not Loaded

FX2-IO17	R202 100	FX2-IO18
FX2-IO19	R203 100	FX2-IO20
FX2-IO21	R204 100	FX2-IO22
FX2-IO23	R205 100	FX2-IO24
FX2-IO25	R206 100	FX2-IO26
FX2-IO27	R207 100	FX2-IO28
FX2-IO35	R208 100	FX2-IO36
FX2-CLKIN	R209 100	FX2-IO38
FX2-IO37	R210 100	FX2-CLKOUT

Spartan 3E 1600 Board	
Digilent Inc. Copyright 2005, 2006	Engineer: CC
SHEET: DDR Memory Signals	Author: GMA
TITLE: S3E-1600	Rev: A
Doc#: 500-100	Date: 3/14/06	Sheet:14/14

Appendix B

Nintendo® NES Gamepad Specifications

‘’ ‘’ ‘’

Controller Features

- General:
    - Model: NES Classic Controller.
    - Type: Gamepad.
    - Compatibility: PC.

- Input:
    - Connectivity: Wired.
    - Buttons: 4-way arrows keypad, 'A' button, 'B' button, 'SELECT' button, and 'START' button.

- Miscellaneous:
    - Color: Black and Gray.
    - Game Consoles Compatibility: Nintendo® NES, Nintendo® Wii, and Nintendo® Wii U.

**Figure (B-1) Nintendo® NES Gamepad (Front)
(Source: uzebox.org).**

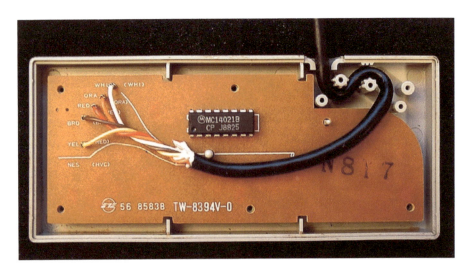

**Figure (B-2) Nintendo® NES Gamepad (Inside)
(Source: uzebox.org).**

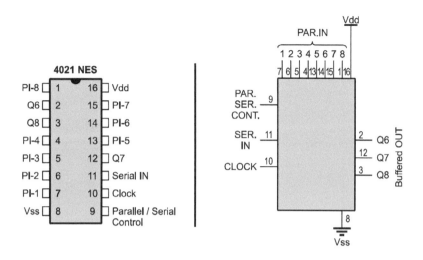

**Figure (B-3) Pinout of 4021 NES Gamepad Chip
(Source: uzebox.org).**

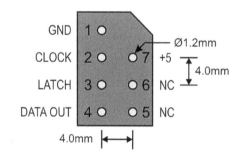

**Figure (B-4) Pinout of NES Gamepad Socket
(Source: spaces.usu.edu).**

Operation	Latch	CLK	CLK	CLK	CLK	CLK	CLK	CLK
	bit 0	bit 1	bit 2	bit 3	bit 4	bit 5	bit 6	bit 7
Data	A	B	Select	Start	Up	Down	Left	Right

**Figure (B-5) Data Format of NES Gamepad
(Source: uzebox.org).**

www.ingramcontent.com/pod-product-compliance
Lightning Source LLC
Chambersburg PA
CBHW041152050326
40690CB00001B/448